Interlopers:
The Difficult People and Life Experiences That Prepare Us for Greater

by
Kenny D. Craig

Copyright © 2021 Kenny D. Craig

Paperback ISBN: 978-1-64719-609-7

Bible passages are quoted from the English Standard Version unless otherwise noted.

All rights reserved. No part of this publication may be reproduced, stored in a retrieval system, or transmitted in any form or by any means, electronic, mechanical, recording or otherwise, without the prior written permission of the author.

Published by BookLocker.com, Inc., St. Petersburg, Florida.

Printed on acid-free paper.

BookLocker.com, Inc.
2021

For Kendall Dylan, Kaleb Daniel, and Kolby Dean, the sons God entrusted into my parentage to train up in the fear and admonition of the Lord and thus make myself a better person.

For Georgia Lee Craig, my maternal grandmother, who sacrificed so much for me when life often left me solely in her care and protection. She gave me Christ because, like the widow in Luke Chapter 21, He was all she had to give; to my benefit, He was more than enough.

For all of my extended family, friends, loved ones, coworkers, and even enemies, who helped shape me though years of interpersonal experience. I would not be who I am without your input and impacts.

Table of Contents

Introduction 1

Dream Killers 3

Ditch Diggers...10

Backstabbers..17

Cell Mates 27

Palace Assignment 39

Lessons from Joseph 54

Foreword

Kenny Craig has preached the Gospel since 1999 and pastored since 2004. His life experiences provide the foundation for this work.

Interlopers: The Difficult People and Life Experiences That Prepare Us for Greater is a book about Joseph. Almost all believers will recognize the name of Joseph. His story has been heard often in Bible study classes and sermons. Many scholars refer to Genesis 37–50 as the "Joseph stories." While the name Joseph is on a brief list of familiar Old Testament characters, Mr. Craig provides rich, fresh insight into this spiritual giant.

Mr. Craig creates practical applications of Joseph's story in chapters entitled "Dream Killers" (Joseph's brothers), "Ditch Diggers" (Joseph cast into a pit), "Backstabbers" (Potiphar's wife), "Cell Mates" (the butler and the baker), and "Palace Assignment" (Joseph elevated in anticipation of a famine).

Mr. Craig defines "interlopers" as those individuals who may prevent Christians from attaining our full potential in Christ. In regard to a back stabber, Mr. Craig writes, "Trust that can take years to build can be shattered with one violation and in many cases, can never be restored. This is the mode of operation of the backstabber." Pertaining to cell mates, Mr. Craig writes that "cell mates are people who don't necessarily add value to our lives; however, they can be the interlopers God uses to help prepare us for a greater cause as we journey through life." In "Palace Assignment," Mr. Craig helps believers realize that God wants to bless his people.

Christians will enjoy Mr. Craig's book. He provides excellent contemporary applications for the lessons presented in the Joseph stories. Readers will see hope throughout the stories of Joseph and throughout this work. This book will make readers want to read and reread the story of Joseph and God's providence.

Mr. Craig reminds believers that "interlopers help prepare us for the greater things assigned to our lives and help transform us to be who God wants us to be when our season of greater arrives." This pastor also helps Christians understand that "the process that leads us from the pit to the palace will ultimately change us in ways we may not have imagined." Christians recognize that the process is important. This book can be a significant part of that process.

R. Kelvin Moore, Th.D.
Professor of Biblical Studies
Union University
Jackson, Tennessee

Interlopers
People who try to stop you from your purpose

INTRODUCTION

Many times in life, we are faced with extreme circumstances and people who don't necessarily have our best interests in mind— but suppose these very same circumstances and people are vital to our growth both spiritually and socially. What if they are actually part of an intricate process that, by design, prepares us for greater things? Although many of us often wish we could experience greatness and excellence, very few have obtained them. The process through which we can be prepared for higher callings and responsibility is directly related to the challenges, obstacles, and even people we encounter on this journey of life. Dictionary.com defines an interloper as an intruder who interferes with, meddles with, or disrupts the affairs of others; Google.com defines an interloper as a person who becomes involved in a place or situation where that person is not wanted or is considered not to belong. God sometimes allows difficult people and painful events to become interlopers into our existence such that in the final summation of those encounters, our lives are so affected that we are better because of the experiences.

Consider a bird that, for several reasons, is unable to migrate south until after the beginning of winter. The bird will have to endure the harshest of conditions and, in some instances, tolerate the extreme elements of nature that often come with winter. If the bird survives, it will undoubtedly learn some valuable life lessons and will be much stronger because of the experience. Many times, our survival in a new crisis can be determined by the lessons we have learned from previous crises, such that the bad experiences that have previously befallen us have really been for our gain. Romans 8:28 (KJV) says, "And we know that all things work together for good to them that love God, to them who are the called according to His purpose."

This book is a journey into the life of Joseph. It chronicles the many horrific tragedies and cruel people he encountered that, through no fault of his own, became interlopers in his life. Even in the worst of these circumstances, God was with Joseph, and these events helped transform and prepare him for a greater destiny. From being a peasant boy tending his father's flock to becoming second-in-command in the palace of Pharaoh, Joseph's experiences, although tragic, were all part of the process that ultimately led to his success. In the end, as he stated in Genesis 50:20, Joseph understood that this process was inclusive of God's plan: "As for you, you meant evil against me, but God meant it for good, to bring it about that many people should be kept alive, as they are today". When we don't understand why we must encounter and deal with difficult people and hardships in life, it is important to remember that a greater life can require from us more than we are sometimes willing to give: "For unto whomsoever much is given, of him shall be much required: and to whom men have committed much, of him they will ask the more" (Luke 12:48). The payoff from these sacrifices far outweigh the temporary discomforts, disappointments, and despairs of life because, ultimately, they lead us to where God has called us.

1

Dream Killers

Now Joseph had a dream, and when he told it to his brothers they hated him even more.

—Genesis 37:5

In this day and time, we are constantly driven toward the pursuit of self-improvement and self-empowerment. A variety of tools are available in the form of books, CDs, motivational speakers, and even life coaches whose sole responsibility is to guide and direct us in making the best life decisions to obtain our goals and dreams. Many times, our dreams and hopes for a better tomorrow fuel our passion as we seek to make our lives better. We often share these dreams and goals with those within our circles of influence, including family, friends, and even coworkers, in hopes that they will become supportive and share in our excitement of these life pursuits. But what happens when we cannot find the hoped-for support? What do we do when those who should be excited for us become envious and even discourage us from following our hearts? How do we cope when the people with whom we have shared our dreams become our dream killers?

Dream killers are people who not only offer us no support as we pursue our dreams but also try to discourage us from pursuing, or even contemplating, the achievement of our dreams. Joseph had a dream, and when he shared it with his brothers, they hated him. We must take and understand a few things from this: First, we must be very careful and selective of whom we share our hopes, goals, desires, aspirations, and dreams with. Revealing our big dreams and our aspirations for greatness can cause our enemies to reveal themselves. People who already don't like us *really* don't like us when we begin to think outside the box and to dream what others deem impossible. The animosity that Joseph's brothers had toward him spawned from jealousy over their father's love of him: "Now Israel loved Joseph more than all his children, because he was the son of his old age: and he made him a coat of many colours. And when his brethren saw that their father loved him more than all his brethren, they hated him, and could not speak peaceably unto him" (Genesis 37:3–4). Prior to sharing his dream with his brothers, Joseph was already disliked not because he had done anything to them but because he was favored by their father.

Have you ever met someone who spoke to you in a harsh tone without cause? Have you ever had to deal with a coworker or colleague who seemed to hold some unjustifiable contempt for you? Many times, people dislike us not because of our actions toward them but simply because we are well liked and beloved by others. We have to understand that some people we encounter will dislike us without cause and cannot speak peacefully to us. These types of people, like Joseph's brothers, dislike us even before we share our dreams with them; unlike Joseph, we should be wary of sharing our dreams and expectations with them because, as Joseph found out, doing so will only make them hate us more. We must therefore not deceive ourselves into believing that everybody will like and appreciate us, because sometimes we are disliked for no reason at all. The challenge for us, then, is to be able to discern between people who genuinely have our best interests at heart and those who do not.

We must also learn from Joseph's encounter with his brothers that dream killers are often not strangers or people foreign to us. Joseph's dream killers were his own flesh-and-blood siblings, who should have been his biggest cheerleaders and support group. It's bad enough when we are mistreated and discouraged by strangers who don't really know us, but when ill will and negative energy come from those whom we classify as family, friends, and loved ones, we can be left scarred for life or severely emotionally damaged. Many times, our biggest hurts and letdowns come from those closest to us. When we understand that blood kinship doesn't automatically equate to loyalty, then the pain and discouragement we feel when our family members become our dream killers won't be so shocking. We may not always admit it, but sometimes, family can be our biggest obstacle to achieving our goals—not because they are inherently evil, but sometimes because their lack of vision and faith can cause them to miss the greatness that resides within their own family. Even Christ was paralyzed by the lack of faith of those from within his own homeland. The potential He had to do great things amongst his own kindred was stymied because of their unbelief: "And Jesus said to them, 'A prophet is not without honor, except in his hometown and among his relatives and in his own household.' And he could do no mighty work there, except that he laid his hands on a few sick people and healed them. And he marveled because of their unbelief. And he went about among the villages teaching" (Mark 6:4–6). Dream killers from amongst our own family can paralyze us simply by not believing in us, which usually results in a lack of support for us. It can be devastating when we cannot turn to the place we call home and find no word of encouragement and no one to help us should we find ourselves in need of motivation.

The last lesson we must take from Joseph's encounter is that the size and audacity of the dream can dictate the amount of contempt from our dream killers. When Joseph shared his dream with his brothers, they hated him even more. Let us consider his dream: "He said to them, 'Hear this dream that I have dreamed: Behold, we were binding sheaves in the field, and behold, my sheaf arose and stood upright. And behold, your sheaves gathered around it and bowed down to my sheaf.' His brothers said to him, 'Are you indeed to reign over us? Or are you indeed to rule over us?' So they hated him even more for his dreams and for his words" (Genesis 37:6–8).

Joseph did not just dream of being the supervisor on the job; he dreamed of owning the company. When we dream beyond the average and aspire to attain more than mediocrity, it can cause some contempt in those around us the likes of which we have never experienced before. As long as we live beneath our potentials, many of those in our circles of influence are content and say nothing about our neutral existences. It's when we have epiphanies that we can do so much more with our lives and therefore actively seek to unlock the greatness within us that our true opposition and dream killers will reveal themselves. You can probably look back over your life to a time when you were not highly motivated and really not doing much. At that time, those in your inner circle probably didn't have much to say about and did not oppose you. The moment you decided to do something better, try something different, and pursue significant change, however, their voices rose in a chorus of naysaying, as they attempted to discourage you from putting much time, effort, or energy into your new goal.

We must be careful of those within our inner circles because, as previously stated, dreaming big and aspiring for greatness can cause the enemies within those circles to reveal themselves. The question Joseph's brothers ask him after he shares his dream is filled with contempt: "Are you indeed to reign and rule over us?" In essence, they are saying, "How dare you say such foolish things! Who do you think you are?" If his dream had been simple and had not elevated him above them, they would not have reacted in such a way and may not have addressed the dream at all.

Joseph also shares with them and their father a second, similar, dream: "Then he dreamed another dream and told it to his brothers and said, 'Behold, I have dreamed another dream. Behold, the sun, the moon, and eleven stars were bowing down to me.' But when he told it to his father and to his brothers, his father rebuked him and said to him, 'What is this dream that you have dreamed? Shall I and your mother and your brothers indeed come to bow ourselves to the ground before you?' And his brothers were jealous of him, but his father kept the saying in mind. And his brothers went to pasture their father's flock near Shechem" (Genesis

37: 9–12). His brothers can no longer stomach being in his presence, so they go to another town to be away from him. Like Joseph, when we have the audacity to hope, the ambition to pursue excellence, the vision to see the unimaginable, and the desire to achieve the spectacular, our enemies and dream killers act accordingly. When we dream big, those who cannot stomach the idea of us doing something significant may leave us. We may find ourselves abandoned and deserted solely for the sake of seeking excellence. The sad reality is some people connected to us have no problem with us as long as we are living no better than they, but the moment we begin to live, act, think, and do better, they become our biggest obstacles. So, when we dream big and outside the parameters of the norm, daring to see ourselves doing great things, we must be careful with whom we share these dreams.

Joseph's dream produced dream killers, who were very close to him. Those closest to him hate him because of the audacity of his dream. What's ironic is that they are livid, filled with rage, over a dream that has not yet come to pass. They have no evidence that it will even take place, meaning it was an un-manifested vision. Like Joseph's brothers, many people are angry, bitter, upset, and even outraged over things that have not even taken place. When you share with them something they themselves cannot imagine, ill feelings, even hatred, are produced because deep down inside, your dream exposes their own inadequacies and shortcomings.

The key for us is to not allow other people's negativity and ill feelings toward us to prevent us from pursuing our goals. We must recognize that no matter how bad these encounters with those opposed to our dreams, the experiences are part of the process that God uses to prepare us for higher callings and greater purposes. Dream killers thus help prepare us for greater destinies.

2

Ditch Diggers

So when Joseph came to his brothers, they stripped him of his robe, the robe of many colors that he wore. And they took him and cast him into a pit. The pit was empty; there was no water in it.

—Genesis 37:23–24

The politics that drive our nation has become divisive and gridlocked to the point that almost nothing is being accomplished for the good of the citizenry. Pick up any newspaper or turn on any twenty-four- hour news channel and you will find vitriol and mean-spirited conduct from both major parties vying for control of the House and Senate. It's disheartening to see individuals go to great lengths to purposefully undermine and orchestrate the destruction of their colleagues simply because they do not agree on certain issues or harbor dislike for them for whatever reasons.

The term *ditch digging* is a metaphor meaning that one is plotting the downfall and failure of another. Ditch diggers, are thus actively digging ditches—seeking the demise of others—by willfully placing those people in positions that will not allow success. Ditch diggers are selfish in nature in that they desire to see no one excel higher or further than themselves. They are peculiar, because they have no loyalty or allegiance to anyone except themselves. They seek only to highlight their own achievements, and they will do anything to tarnish the achievements of others if that will elevate their own even more.

Having found no support within his family after sharing his dream, Joseph finds himself thrown into a terrible situation. His brothers have gone to another town to be away from him, but Joseph's father sends him to check on them: "And Israel said to Joseph, 'Are not your brothers pasturing the flock at Shechem? Come, I will send you to them.' And he said to him, 'Here I am.' So he said to him, 'Go now, see if it is well with your brothers and with the flock, and bring me word.' So he sent him from the Valley of Hebron, and he came to Shechem" (Genesis 37:13–14).

As Joseph is making his way to find his brothers, they see him coming from a distance and conspire to kill him: "They saw him from afar, and before he came near to them they conspired against him to kill him. They said to one another, 'Here comes this dreamer. Come now, let us kill him and throw him into one of the pits. Then we will say that a fierce animal has devoured him, and we will see what will become of his dreams' " (Genesis 37:18–20). This is disturbing for several reasons. First is because they see him coming to check on them, not coming to them with ill will or malice. In fact, he is doing something good on his father's behalf by checking on their well-being.

As with Joseph's brothers, our ditch diggers can see us coming from afar, meaning they can see the good we are doing and still conspire against us. Truthfully, it's this good about us that they cannot handle. We must understand that some people cannot tolerate the good in us because there is something void or lacking within them. The challenge for us is to recognize that no matter how much good we do, how kind we are, or how much of ourselves we sacrifice, someone will still not be pleased. We must remember that such a person's dislike of us is not really about us but rather about our achieving or accomplishing something good. Ditch diggers don't want to see anyone else do a good work, especially if they are not part of the process.

Joseph's brothers see an opportunity not only to stop Joseph's dream from happening but also to literally kill him. In this way, they are prime examples of how ditch diggers take dream killing one step further: They are not satisfied with blocking our progress but are intent on our total destruction. They don't want to see you demoted from a position; they desire to see you fired from the job.

The second reason that the behavior of Joseph's brothers is disturbing is that they conspire together against him. Many times, people will get together to plot and plan against us. It's cliché, but it's true for ditch diggers: An enemy of my enemy is my friend. The brothers share a common hatred for Joseph and therefore enter into an agreement to kill him. You may have experienced multiple people promoting an untruth or misinformation about you in order that you might fail. Perhaps several coworkers conspired together and twisted what was true for their own gain while you took the fall and ultimately had to find employment elsewhere. Although Joseph knew all of his ditch diggers, you may not know all of yours, because people don't have to know you personally to conspire against you—their common goal to destroy something in your life. This is why rumors and gossip are so easily believed and passed from one person to the next. Sometimes, people participate unknowingly in the downfall of others simply by perpetuating information they do not know to be true.

The last disturbing thing we see in this scene is that Joseph's brothers decide that after killing him, they will create a story that he was killed by a wild animal. Ditch diggers will always attempt to make a mockery of you and of anything you have accomplished. Such people do not allow us to outlive our pasts; no matter how we may have turned our lives around or changed for the good, they find ways to attach our past mistakes and misfortunes to our current progress.

If they are not attaching our pasts to our present, ditch diggers seek to find something wrong with whatever we do; they love to make mockeries of us by spreading criticism—no matter how trivial or petty—of us as often as possible, to anyone who will listen. Joseph's brothers are not satisfied with planning his death but also decide to make a mockery of him by misrepresenting the truth surrounding his death. If we should happen to fall into ditches of life, there will be those who will relish making mockeries of us by misrepresenting the truth.

As tragic as the plotting by Joseph's brothers is, there is still a bit of hope, as one of the brothers—Reuben—convinces the others not to kill Joseph but rather to put him in a pit so he might succumb to natural death: "And Reuben said to them, 'Shed no blood; cast him into this pit here in the wilderness, but do not lay a hand on him'—that he might rescue him out of their hand to restore him to his father. So, when Joseph came to his brothers, they stripped him of his robe, the robe of many colors that he wore. And they took him and cast him into a pit. The pit was empty; there was no water in it" (Genesis 37:22–24).

Here, we should be encouraged, because although being thrown into a pit is a horrible experience for Joseph, it does not kill him as his brothers had intended. As He did with this plan, God has a way of thwarting our enemies' plans. They may plot and even carry out their plans for our destruction, but in the end, neither they nor their plans can kill us; they ultimately disrupt our lives, not realizing that God is using them to advance us for a greater good.

The fact that the pit his brothers throw Joseph in contains no water is significant, because it means he cannot drown. Thus, though the pit was chosen as a place for him to die, it actually guaranteed he would live. We must recognize that, similarly, no matter how deep or wide are the ditches dug for us, they are necessary to the process that God uses to prepare us for higher callings and greater purposes.

Joseph's brother Reuben has convinced his fellow brethren not to kill Joseph; it is his plan to rescue Joseph and deliver him back to their father before any harm could come to Joseph. Before Reuben could return to save Joseph, however, the other brothers seize an opportunity to sell Joseph to a band of Ishmaelites from Gilead for twenty pieces of silver: "Then Midianite traders passed by. And they drew Joseph up and lifted him out of the pit, and sold him to the Ishmaelites for twenty shekels of silver. They took Joseph to Egypt" (Genesis 37:28).

Here is their chance to be rid of their brother and to profit off him at the same time. Like Joseph's brothers, so intent on being rid of their brother that they sell him for a few pieces of silver, ditch diggers will sell you out if the opportunity presents itself. Jesus himself knew how those within our inner circles can sell us out if the opportunity presents itself: "And the chief priests and scribes sought how they might kill him; for they feared the people. Then entered Satan into Judas surnamed Iscariot, being of the number of the twelve. And he went his way, and communed with the chief priests and captains, how he might betray him unto them. And they were glad, and covenanted to give him money. And he promised, and sought opportunity to betray him unto them in the absence of the multitude" (Luke 22:2–6).

Those who set traps for us will do so in order that they might gain from the experience. In many cities throughout our nation, law enforcement agencies set up anonymous hotlines whereby individuals (including those considered friends) can call in with information about crimes committed, and if the reported party is arrested, the person who phoned in the tip receives a monetary reward. This system is beneficial for both the communities and police officials because it allows those willing to give information to make a profit and rid their communities of the lawbreakers at the same time. It's important to understand that people in our lives can sell us out for many things other than money including jobs, promotions, influence, power, and even our own possessions. The more you accomplish, the greater the possibility of a setup by a ditch digger who desires the prestige of the position you occupy.

After selling Joseph, his brothers dip his coat of many colors in animal's blood, then take it back to their father so he will reach the conclusion that Joseph was killed by a wild beast. As strange as it may seem, some individuals, like Joseph's brothers, relish misrepresenting the truth of our misfortunes so others, misinformed, thus reach conclusions that are far from the truth. Many times, people count us out and pass judgment on us because of on lies, deceit, and recasting of the truth by the ditch digger.

The blessing in the scripture is that although Joseph is sold to a band of merchants, he is ultimately taken to Egypt, away from the pit that was purposed to kill him: "Meanwhile the Midianites had sold him in Egypt to Potiphar, an officer of Pharaoh, the captain of the guard" (Genesis 37:36). In a similar way, God repurposes the vile and sometimes treacherous purposes of the ditch digger for His own glory, ultimately preparing us for greater futures in ways we could have never imagined. Ditch diggers thus help prepare us for greater destinies.

3

Backstabbers

She caught him by his garment, saying, "Lie with me." But he left his garment in her hand and fled and got out of the house. And as soon as she saw that he had left his garment in her hand and had fled out of the house, she called to the men of her household and said to them, "See, he has brought among us a Hebrew to laugh at us. He came in to me to lie with me, and I cried out with a loud voice. And as soon as he heard that I lifted up my voice and cried out, he left his garment beside me and fled and got out of the house." Then she laid up his garment by her until his master came home.

–Genesis 39:12-16

Suzanne Collins, author of *The Hunger Games,* once stated, "For there to be betrayal, there would have to have been trust first." Betrayal is a violation of trust in some form or another. It's this breach of trust that has caused much devastation and destruction to kinships, friendships, and relationships. Either by intent or without malice, a violation of trust can result in the ultimate separation of bonds between people. Trust that took years to build can be shattered with one violation and in many cases, can never be restored.

Backstabbers betray others, either directly or indirectly, to accomplish their own selfish goals, often leaving others to pay for their actions. They tend to do things behind our backs and without our knowledge. This betrayal can alter the course of our lives. In most cases, the backstabber violates or misuses a trust that has taken a great length of time to establish, though violation of trust between those who have known each other only briefly can be just as damaging. In either case, back stabbing often has horrific consequences. It's these consequences that can become interlopers in and alter our lives.

Joseph's life course has been drastically altered by the betrayal of his brothers. He was sent to his brothers as a shepherd boy among family but departs from them as a slave among strangers, and was sold a second time to a high-ranking officer of Pharaoh: "Now Joseph had been brought down to Egypt, and Potiphar, an officer of Pharaoh, the captain of the guard, an Egyptian, had bought him from the Ishmaelites who had brought him down there" (Genesis 39:1).

It's easy to become discouraged after reading this passage, because it seems as if life has a way of selling us and reselling us again and again, as if after we have suffered one difficult moment, we are subjected to yet another. Many people, after dealing with one mishap after another, asked, *Why me?* Others often utter the cliché *When it rains, it pours.*

The good news is that despite what happened to Joseph, the Lord was with him:

> *The Lord was with Joseph, and he became a successful man, and he was in the house of his Egyptian master. His master saw that the Lord was with him and that the Lord caused all that he did to succeed in his hands. So Joseph found favor in his sight and attended him, and he made him overseer of his house and put him in charge of all that he had. From the*

time that he made him overseer in his house and over all that he had the Lord blessed the Egyptian's house for Joseph's sake; the blessing of the Lord was on all that he had, in house and field. So he left all that he had in Joseph's charge, and because of him he had no concern about anything but the food he ate.

(Genesis 39:2–6)

The first verse of this passage can be difficult for many to understand, yet alone believe. Some people consider the idea that God is with us during our darkest hours laughable, even oxymoronic. Many people have the erroneous mindset that God is with us only during our brightest moments. The question that must be asked, especially of those of us who acknowledge a personal relationship with the Lord, is *Can you see Him when life leaves you, like Joseph, living as a slave among strangers?* It can be a challenge to see Christ in your life when you are living in captivity, but this text clearly demonstrates that God was with Joseph even when Joseph was a slave: God made it so Joseph was living as well as, if not better than, any free man. Potiphar, the officer of Pharaoh, saw that the Lord was with Joseph. This is fascinating because it's a revelation of the attitude and character that Joseph must have displayed during difficult moments. We must understand that sometimes the key to surviving our captivity can be found in our attitude and character rather than in ingenious escape plans. When we allow the Lord to have free rein in our hearts, it is reflected in the way we respond to our crises and will be clear to others, such that they too will acknowledge the presence of God with us, as Joseph's captor, Potiphar, did.

We should take notice of Joseph's humility. The Bible makes no reference to Joseph returning the hate and the venom that his brothers had displayed toward him. He did not become confrontational with his father when he too discounted his dream. Not once did Joseph mistreat, fight, or disrespect the Midianites who purchased him, and when he is sold again to Potiphar, he goes willingly and does humbly what is asked or commanded of him. His spirit, humility, and gentle nature thus lead his captor to conclude that the Lord was with Joseph.

We should note here that the Lord blessed Joseph while he was still a captive. We must therefore not assume that the Lord is using us or doing good with us only when everything is going well for us. The Lord can and will bless you in ways you cannot imagine, even when you are in exigent circumstances. When he was initially sold and resold, Joseph did not foresee himself being placed over all the affairs of a high-ranking official of the king's court, nor that servants would be answering to him. It's thus critical that before we engage in self-loathing and self-pity, we remember that nothing is impossible with God. In fact, our worst times can become our best times when we learn to see God working on our behalf within the confines of our crises. Joseph could have dwelled on the fact that he was still a slave, but instead, he moved forward knowing he was in charge. We can take from this that the way we respond to a crisis can often dictate how free we become. Joseph was not released by Potiphar from his captivity but was placed as overseer of Potiphar's entire household and all that he had. Can you imagine that? A slave was completely in charge of all the affairs of his master!

When we understand that our captivity has a purpose, we, like Joseph, can be free within that captivity. Our circumstances may not change, but when the Lord is with us, we have freedom, nonetheless. You may know someone who has experienced a traumatic event yet who genuinely displays the joy of the Lord and glorifies God in spite of that event. Perhaps you have encountered someone sick to the point of death who left you feeling blessed, encouraged, and uplifted after the encounter. This is the type of freedom Joseph experiences in his captivity under Potiphar.

Now that things are beginning to get better for Joseph and the outlook for his captivity had begun to change for the better, however, another interloper presents itself. Potiphar's wife sets her sights on Joseph and desires to have an illicit adulterous affair with him, but Joseph refuses her attempts to get him to betray God and Potiphar, to whom he is loyal: "And after a time his master's wife cast her eyes on Joseph and said, 'Lie with me.' But he refused and said to his master's wife, 'Behold, because of me my master has no concern about anything in the house, and he has put everything that he has in my charge. He is not greater in this house than I am, nor has he kept back anything from me except yourself, because you are his wife. How then can I do this great wickedness and sin against God?' " (Genesis 39:7–9). Joseph is in a terrible predicament. Potiphar's wife is intent on getting Joseph to go along with her plan and to thus betray his master.

The relationship between the two is conditional based on the appointment of Joseph over Potiphar's home: Because of his relationship with Potiphar, Joseph must occasionally come in contact with Potiphar's wife. Like Potiphar's wife, backstabbers tend to be conditional to our relationships and can come into our lives without our permission or choice. For example, we may be assigned relationships by appointment, such as with a new job, school, or relocation. Then there are relationships we select, allowing others to come into our lives as friends, spouses, or professionals, such as doctors and lawyers. Both appointed and selected relationships can be unraveled by an act of betrayal. Backstabbers will use us if it suits their purposes, even if it will cause us to betray others. Potiphar's wife didn't care about Joseph's relationship with her husband or with God and therefore pressured him to accomplish her own goal. Young people often experience this in the form of peer pressure, pressured to try various substances or to perform certain acts, only to betray themselves, their parents, the law, and their God.

The telltale sign of the backstabber is that they couldn't care less about the feelings of those they are pressuring. Even after Joseph explains that he could not betray his master or his God, Potiphar's wife harasses and pressures him daily to reconsider and give in: "And as she spoke to Joseph day after day, he would not listen to her, to lie beside her or to be with her" (Genesis 39:10). If we find ourselves pressured by those we think are our friends even after we have expressed our desire not to do what they are asking, we must conclude that they are backstabbers and have betrayed our friendship and we should consider ending this unhealthy relationship. The tragedy is that all too often, people try to remain loyal to backstabbers because they are unwilling to disconnect themselves even from people who would betray them. Thus, the very ones they seek validation from become the very ones who pressure them to make bad choices.

Potiphar's wife is convinced that if the opportunity is available and the temptation strong enough, Joseph will give in, so she cunningly sends all the servants away so she will have her chance to get what she seeks: "But one day, when he went into the house to do his work and none of the men of the house was there in the house . . . " (Genesis 39:11). It's interesting to note here that no servants or attendants were present in the house, which is vacant except for Mrs. Potiphar. Although it's not stated in the text, we can assume that she has given everyone the day off without Joseph's permission! Joseph is second-in-command to Potiphar, and all the servants and household attendants must report to him, especially on matters dealing with absence, yet on this particular day, He goes to work and finds none of the employees there.

Potiphar's wife immediately grabs Joseph, demanding he sleep with her: "she caught him by his garment, saying, 'Lie with me.' But he left his garment in her hand and fled and got out of the house" (Genesis 39:12). Joseph has finally had enough of Potiphar's wife's advances, and he removes himself from an inappropriate moment, leaving the house altogether. He has no choice but to take drastic matters because she has planned for him to fail and to betray those to whom he is loyal.

Like Mrs. Potiphar, backstabbers will seek to find the right opportunity to place us in uncomfortable situations, hoping that we will give in to their wants and desires. The situation can be something as seemingly harmless as them asking an uncomfortable question in front of others or as serious as threatening to expose a secret. Either way, the intended goal is to force us to do their will without any regard or thought to us.

Joseph flees from his master's wife, leaving his garment behind. Following Joseph's lead, we must not live in denial when dealing with backstabbers and should flee such relationships at all costs, leaving behind anything associated with them. We should not allow anyone to misuse or abuse our relationships.

The sad reality is that when Mrs. Potiphar couldn't get Joseph to betray her husband, she betrays Joseph: "Then she laid up his garment by her until his master came home, and she told him the same story, saying, 'The Hebrew servant, whom you have brought among us, came in to me to laugh at me. But as soon as I lifted up my voice and cried, he left his garment beside me and fled out of the house.' As soon as his master heard the words that his wife spoke to him, 'This is the way your servant treated me,' his anger was kindled. And Joseph's master took him and put him into the prison, the place where the king's prisoners were confined, and he was there in prison" (Genesis 39:16–20).

Potiphar's wife has stabbed Joseph in the back by concocting a story alleging that he tried to rape her when, in fact, the exact opposite is true and she is guilty of the allegations she is making against him. When backstabbers turn on you, they will attempt to make the lie a truth and the truth a lie. They revel in hypocrisy, accusing others of the acts they themselves are guilty of, they will use whatever means available to betray those whom they cannot manipulate, often with severe consequences. Because of his wife's betrayal and lies, Potiphar has Joseph arrested and thrown in prison.

We see no dialogue take place between the two men, which suggests that Potiphar passes judgment on Joseph without knowing his side of the story. This is a common occurrence in our society today: People will write us off and throw us away based on hearsay and the false accusations of others without ever knowing our side of the story. We can assume that Potiphar never considers having a conversation with Joseph to ascertain, at the very least, the reason behind the alleged betrayal. Potiphar thus keeps himself in the dark about the *real* infidelity and betrayal—that of his wife.

As this story shows us, multiple people are often victims of backstabbers' treachery and, as in this case, are used to injure or mistreat another victim. Unbeknown to him, Potiphar is a victim of his wife's ill intent, and because he chooses not to gather all the facts concerning this incident, he mistreats the very one who has been truly loyal to him and severs that relationship. Backstabbers can and will destroy the relationships of others if it can benefit or protect them. They will always seek to preserve themselves at the expense of others if need be. Years of friendship and trust can thus be instantly destroyed at the hand of a backstabber.

Backstabbers help prepare us for greatness because their works come unannounced and force us in directions we never planned to go—in directions God wants us to travel. So, while it appears that someone else has forced a change in the course of our lives, it's actually by divine design so God's will can be accomplished in us. Those who seek to destroy us or our relationships with others may thus actually lead us down the path of greatness. For example, Joseph is thrown into prison, his life taking yet another unforeseen turn just when it appears he was doing well. Joseph and Potiphar have become so close and Joseph is so loyal to Potiphar that he has no idea that he needs to be separated from Potiphar. God, however, understands that Joseph will never reach the greatness God has planned for him because Joseph will never leave Potiphar's house on his own.

Many times, we limit ourselves by becoming so close and loyal to people that we can never fully walk into the greater life that God has planned for us, because, like Joseph, we would never leave those people or our places in their lives. God allowed and used the actions of Mrs. Potiphar to cause a breach in the relationship of Joseph and Potiphar so He could continue leading Joseph to the place He intended for Joseph. Joseph could not envision himself in the palace because he was so loyal to Potiphar.

The lesson here: Don't be afraid to lose people on your way to greater things. Sometimes they will have to leave you, and sometimes you will have to leave them, but such loss is necessary and in the end, will be for your good. We must understand that not everyone can or is intended to make the entire journey with us. There will be Potiphars in our lives—people who will discard us and never look back. When we are discarded, we must remind ourselves that they were never intended to enter into our greatness with us, and we should celebrate the idea that God thinks enough of us that he weeds out of our lives the folks who could and would be detrimental to the greater things that await us.

4

Cell Mates

And Joseph's master took him, and put him into the prison, a place where the king's prisoners were bound: and he was there in the prison. . . . And Pharaoh was wroth against two of his officers, against the chief of the butlers, and against the chief of the bakers. And he put them in ward in the house of the captain of the guard, into the prison, the place where Joseph was bound.

—Genesis 39:20; 40:2

Some, if not many, people in our lives add no value to them. In some ways, it's as if we are just doing time with these people, like cell mates in prison. A prime example can be seen in the people we have consistent interactions with but are not intimately connected to, including coworkers, employees at our local grocery store, and even our mail carriers.

Cell mates are not necessarily our friends; however, they are not necessarily our enemies, either. The circumstances that bring cell mates together can vary but are really irrelevant to our discussion here. The point is that we and our cell mates just do time together in life until circumstances remove one or both parties from this block of shared time.

Over time, cell mates can influence us or be influenced by us. Cell mates don't necessarily add value to our lives but can be interlopers used by God to help prepare us for greater causes as we journey through life. God can use them in our lives through chance meetings or random encounters to shift us in the direction He has destined for us. What's unique about these interlopers is that in most instances, they do not arrive in our lives by their own or our plans and do not come with ulterior motives or hidden agendas. God allows us or causes us to cross paths with certain people for the sole purpose of creating an impression, perception, or understanding with them that can result in positive consequences. Many people have obtained new jobs or careers because of chance meetings with CEOs. Others have found true love and happiness because of random encounters with people they didn't previously know. Still others have gained insight and revelation about a particular subject matter simply because they were at the right place at the right time.

Joseph has been imprisoned through no fault of his own. This in itself is a travesty, and most people in Joseph's shoes at this point would give up hope and lose faith in God. It can be difficult to remain positive when negative things keep happening to us. Countless people have committed suicide, have begun using drugs or alcohol, or have engaged in other illicit behaviors because they have given up hope, succumbing to the frustrations of a life plagued with one bad incident after another.

It can be very difficult to see what God has planned for us at the palace while we are confined in prison. This is why we must not allow our external circumstances to define who we are and what God can do. God is with us even in the worst of times and can bless us even while we are going through prison, as Joseph found out: "And Joseph's master took him, and put him into the prison, a place where the king's prisoners were bound: and he was there in the prison. But the Lord was with Joseph, and shewed him mercy, and gave him favour in the sight of the keeper of the prison. And the keeper of the prison committed to Joseph's hand all the prisoners that were in the prison; and whatsoever they did there, he was the doer of it. The keeper of the prison looked not to anything that was under his hand; because the Lord was with him, and that which he did, the Lord made it to prosper" (Genesis 39:20–23). This passage serves to remind us that we can be in bondage yet remain completely free. Although Joseph is bound by prison walls, he has freedom in God to be the master of his captivity.

Many things can leave us in bondage, such as sickness, bills, careers, lifestyle, and even relationships. If we can grasp the idea that, like Joseph, we can master those things that bind us, God will give us freedom while we are yet in bondage. The scripture says that the keeper of the prison made Joseph the overseer of all the inmates there! Can you imagine being incarcerated in prison but being given the keys and full authority over the day-to-day operations of the facility? This is supposed to be a place of punishment and misery for the crimes Joseph allegedly committed, yet God gives Joseph favor with the very person who was supposed to lock him up, allowing Joseph freedom in his prison. We must not miss this prolific statement of principle: God can repurpose and reposition people's roles in our lives so those who are meant by man to keep us bound actually help us walk in our freedom.

Again, we must take note of Joseph's humility. Although he has found favor with God during terrible circumstances, he does not abuse or misuse his blessing. He could have easily become a tyrant, forcing everybody under his control to do his bidding while he sat back and enjoyed the good life—but the Scripture says that whatsoever the other prisoners did while there, Joseph also did. In other words, there was no physical labor the prisoners were subjected to that he did not do also. Joseph understood that people enduring hardships cannot be reached by those whom they perceive as not understanding their plight.

Joseph's behavior in prison suggests that he doesn't cast judgment on those in the same situation as him just because he has been elevated to a higher position. People who are destined for greater destinies have learned to relate to people and feel compassion for others. All too often, people in positions of authority are disconnected from or dismissive of the conditions of those they have authority over and have no real sense of compassion for them. How many supervisors are harsh and cruel toward people they once worked with, now that they have been elevated to a higher position? How quickly some people forget what it was like to work alongside the very ones they are now over! Joseph's display of humility even in the worst of life's mishaps causes him to be blessed of God and to prosper while still in bondage: "because the Lord was with him . . . that which he did, the Lord made it to prosper" (Genesis 39:23).

Like Joseph, those who are destined for greater things learn to be content with where they are in life because they understand that things can change. They know that ultimately, God is in control, as Paul explains in Philippians 4:11–12: "for I have learned, in whatsoever state I am, therewith to be content. I know both how to be abased, and I know how to abound: everywhere and in all things I am instructed both to be full and to be hungry, both to abound and to suffer need." When we learn to be content and humble in spite of our circumstances, we allow God to begin working things out on our behalf.

Unbeknown to Joseph, who is laboring in the prison, Pharaoh has become upset with his chief butler and chief baker at the palace and, in his rage, has cast them into the prison where Joseph is in command: "And Pharaoh was wroth against two of his officers, against the chief of the butlers, and against the chief of the bakers. And he put them in ward in the house of the captain of the guard, into the prison, the place where Joseph was bound. And the captain of the guard charged Joseph with them, and he served them: and they continued a season in ward" (Genesis 40:2-3-4). What's amazing here is that God can interweave two seemingly isolated incidents to allow meetings of cell mates to take place. The baker and butler are cast into prison, but because they are personal servants of Pharaoh, they are considered higher in class than the other prisoners and are therefore assigned Joseph to personally serve them until their punishment is over.

The Scripture says the three are placed together for a season in the prison. This is important to note because cell mates are assigned to us for only a season. Whether the season is one day or one year, when the season expires, our assignment together is complete. Many people suffer in relationships because they are clinging to relationships that, like milk, have expiration dates. God purposely place our paths to connect with people whom we would have never have met on our own, so His purpose for our lives can be fulfilled.

Make no mistake: It is not by coincidence that Pharaoh's personal servants are assigned to Joseph for their upkeep and maintenance. It's also no coincidence that you have met and dealt with people who were in your life for only a season. We must be wise enough to accept when that season is over and to not allow misguided emotions to cause us to cling to people whom God never purposed as permanent in our lives.

One night while they continued this assigned season together, both the servants of Pharaoh had a dream. When Joseph came the next morning to attend to them, he noticed their sad countenances and asked what was wrong. They were sad because the dream greatly disturbed them but they had no one to interpret it for them while they were incarcerated: "And Joseph came in unto them in the morning, and looked upon them, and, behold, they were sad. And he asked Pharaoh's officers that were with him in the ward of his lord's house, saying, Wherefore look ye so sadly today? And they said unto him, We have dreamed a dream, and there is no interpreter of it. And Joseph said unto them, Do not interpretations belong to God? Tell me them, I pray you" (Genesis 40:6–8).

Again, we see Joseph's character on display. He could have expressed his sympathies for the servants of Pharaoh and gone on about his daily chores, but instead, Joseph uses this opportunity to help those in distress in spite of his own incarceration. People who are on a path to greater things often have the ability to push aside their own dilemmas so they can help others navigate theirs. Joseph understood that his external condition did not prevent him from being who he was.

It is critical that, like Joseph, we learn how to master normalcy amid our chaos. People who are helpful are generally helpful no matter what may be taking place around them. Joseph disregards his own burden of imprisonment and assignment as personal attendant to Pharaoh's servants. He asks them to share their dream, that he might interpret it and thereby bring them relief and answers.

It is important to note here the question that Joseph asks the men: *Do not interpretations belong to God?* The ability to rely on their faith is typical of those who have the potential to achieve greatness. Joseph understood that because of his own incarceration, his ability to really help these men with their struggle was limited, but he also understood, as people of faith commonly do, that in some instances, the interpretations of our issues should be left for God alone.

When Joseph asks the two servants of Pharaoh to tell him about their dream, the butler speaks up while the baker remains silent. After the butler shares his dream, Joseph gives a favorable interpretation of the dream, asking only that the butler remember this kind gesture when he is restored to his position of influence with Pharaoh and might remove Joseph from prison: "Then Joseph said to him, 'This is its interpretation: the three branches are three days. In three days Pharaoh will lift up your head and restore you to your office, and you shall place Pharaoh's cup in his hand as formerly, when you were his cupbearer. Only remember me, when it is well with you, and please do me the kindness to mention me to Pharaoh, and so get me out of this house. For I was indeed stolen out of the land of the Hebrews, and here also I have done nothing that they should put me into the pit' " (Genesis 40:12–15).

Here, for the first time, we see Joseph's desire to be out of his prison. At no other time has he asked or petitioned for his freedom, but here, he takes an opportunity to seek the assistance of the butler for his own assistance. At first glance, it might appear that Joseph helped the butler only because he had a hidden agenda. Some might argue that Joseph is using this opportunity as quid pro quo in a selfish attempt to be free, but a deeper look shows us that Joseph actually had an epiphany: For the first time since he began experiencing one mishap after another, he can actually see himself free! Joseph now understands that, just as life has misfortunes, it also has opportunities.

The challenge for us, then is to have the ability to see ourselves free from our circumstances. The truth of the matter is that if you can't see yourself doing better, you probably *won't* do better. Think about it: Can you see yourself free of your dilemma? Can you see yourself debt-free? Can you see yourself as the next CEO of your company? Can you see yourself where you desire to be? If you cannot visualize it, you will not actualize it.

Those on journeys to greatness have learned to see the achievement before they have obtained it. Joseph sees his cell mate as an opportunity that can lead to his freedom. It's imperative for us to understand this concept. God will allow us to cross paths with individuals for a season to create opportunities that could lead to our freedom from the difficulties imprisoning us.

We must note that even in Joseph's request to the butler, however, Joseph remains as humble as ever. He does not demand or threaten the butler but simply asks the butler to remember him and to mention his name in kindness to Pharaoh, who has the authority to release him. Even when we see the possibility of an opportunity to be free of our dilemmas, we must remain humble as we pursue them. Sometimes people become exhausted and frustrated with their prison cells and seek solutions in the wrong spirit. When people become desperate to climb the ladder to reach the highest position, they often become abusive, demanding, inconsiderate, and even deceitful in order to get there. Joseph understood that taking this tone with a servant of Pharaoh would not get him anywhere, however.

What takes place next is interesting. After this exchange between Joseph and the butler, the baker does something common among cell mates: "When the chief baker saw that the interpretation was good, he said unto Joseph, I also was in my dream, and, behold, I had three white baskets on my head" (Genesis 40:16). Remember that when Joseph first invited the two men to share their dream, the baker did not speak up immediately but remained silent. Only when the baker sees that the interpretation of the butler's dream is good does he decides to seek Joseph's assistance.

We must be careful when dealing with those in our lives like the baker. This type of cell mate may look for and seek opportunities to use us for their own selfish gains, as the baker in not speaking up until after he heard Joseph's favorable interpretation of the butler dream. It's crucial for us to understand that some people will sit in our circles in silence until they perceive that we can benefit them or advance their causes. You may have experienced people you have known for a time become overly kind to you suddenly and without cause, initiating conversations with you consistently even though previously, they had very little to say. We should exercise caution when those with whom we have no usual interactions begin to include us as if we have been connected to them for years. There is nothing wrong with meeting new people and making new friends, but those whom we have known for a time but who have never tried to become friends should cause us to consider their reason behind the sudden shift to become involved in our lives. The baker comes to Joseph not because he considers Joseph a friend but because he desires to receive the same good news as the butler. Josephs interpretation of his dream interpretation is not so pleasant, however: "And Joseph answered and said, This is the interpretation thereof: The three baskets are three days: Yet within three days shall Pharaoh lift up thy head from off thee, and shall hang thee on a tree; and the birds shall eat thy flesh from off thee" (Genesis 40:18–19). Joseph does not allow the baker's newfound interest in him to prevent him from speaking truth nor alter who he is, as we sometimes do to be accepted by others.

Our youth are especially vulnerable to peer pressure because of the need to be accepted and befriended by those who are popular or well known. Although previously rejected, unaccepted, or perhaps even excluded by those cell mates in their lives, some youth will mistake newly placed attention as acceptance and thus will not speak the truth when it is needed and may even alter who they are or change their behavior just to fit in. Joseph does the opposite. He remains true to himself and speaks truth to the baker, who was seeking to gain his attention. We don't have to change who we are to be accepted by others, nor should we fail to be honest and upfront with people who seek to be active in our lives. People on a path to greatness are not willing to sacrifice their integrity just to fit in.

When Joseph's season with his cell mates ends, he is still in prison, with no freedom in sight: "And it came to pass the third day, which was Pharaoh's birthday, that he made a feast unto all his servants: and he lifted up the head of the chief butler and of the chief baker among his servants. And he restored the chief butler unto his butlership again; and he gave the cup into Pharaoh's hand: But he hanged the chief baker: as Joseph had interpreted to them. Yet did not the chief butler remember Joseph, but forgat him" (Genesis 40:20–23). As previously stated, cell mates are temporary by design and hold no real permanency in our lives. Joseph was ultimately not any better before the servants of Pharaoh were assigned to him or after they departed his experience. The sad reality is that even after he has added value to their lives, they've added none to his.

This scripture reminds us of an all too familiar scenario: We help those who are in need, yet when we seek their assistance, they forget about us. It would seem that as soon as the chief butler was restored by the hand of Pharaoh to his position just as Joseph declared, he should remember Joseph, immediately speaking to Pharaoh to have Joseph released from prison. Sadly, however, he forgets Joseph and how Joseph attended to his needs while he was in prison. We have no guarantee that cell mates will remember our kindness and charitable deeds toward them when our season together expires; thus, we should never pin our hopes and dreams for desired outcomes on the benevolence of others. Although God uses cell mates as interlopers to create opportunity to lead us toward the things in store for us, it is not necessarily on the timetable we assume.

The fact that the butler forgets about Joseph is irrelevant, because their season together created the opportunity for the seed of destination to be planted. Joseph has no idea that what God has in store for him has already been accomplished, because no immediate change to Joseph's confinement occurs after the season with his cell mates has ended. Sometimes we miss what God has done because we are still living in the here and now, as Joseph did in this case. For this reason, we must never relinquish our faith based on what we see in the here and now. Although our confinement to life's difficulties may not immediately change, it does not mean God's purpose has not been accomplished, as we will see in Joseph's life in the next chapter.

5

Palace Assignment

Then Pharaoh said to Joseph, "Since God has shown you all this, there is none so discerning and wise as you are. You shall be over my house, and all my people shall order themselves as you command. Only as regards the throne will I be greater than you." And Pharaoh said to Joseph, "See, I have set you over all the land of Egypt." Then Pharaoh took his signet ring from his hand and put it on Joseph's hand, and clothed him in garments of fine linen and put a gold chain about his neck. And he made him ride in his second chariot. And they called out before him, "Bow the knee!" Thus he set him over all the land of Egypt. Moreover, Pharaoh said to Joseph, "I am Pharaoh, and without your consent no one shall lift up hand or foot in all the land of Egypt.

—Genesis 41:39–44

There is an adage that says, "What God has for me is for me." Although the idea may seem foreign to some, others understand the saying firsthand. Some things we have obtained or achieved in life can be credited to God alone. If we are completely honest with ourselves, we have to admit that we own some property that perhaps our credit would suggest we shouldn't be allowed to, we are in positions that our experience or education levels do not qualify us for, or we hold some influence that we should not, based on our name or status. Because of who God is, however, we are not necessarily limited to obtaining and achieving greatness in the way that society might require. We should understand that blessings are not really about us but are completely about God. We believers understand that God doesn't need mankind's permission to elevate or promote us to positions of power or influence. When we have the favor of God, He will supersede the requirements of man and society.

When we understand this, we can understand that even ordinary people can be on journeys toward extraordinary things. We have many examples throughout history of the least of our society accomplishing great things even in spite of tremendous opposition. When God has greater things in store for us, He often uses interlopers to lead us down His path to accomplish His ends, as he does with the butler in Joseph's life.

Joseph, still in prison, has been forgotten by the butler he served and whom he helped through a struggle. What we must take from this is that although man may forget about us when we are in need, God never does. Though we may think this a tragedy for Joseph, we soon learn that all happens in God's time: "After two whole years, Pharaoh dreamed that he was standing by the Nile" (Genesis 41:1).

It is true that the butler forgot Joseph—but it was by divine intent, not man's neglect. Notice that the Pharaoh had no dream of significance for two years. This is key to Joseph's story because although the butler did forget about him, for two years had no need or reason to remember since the Pharaoh never summons him on matters concerning dreams. Many times, we get frustrated with God because He does not immediately respond to our crises or remove our difficulties—but it's important that we remember that God will not always respond to our pleas immediately. Though our blessings and outcomes may be delayed on the path toward greater things, that does not mean they are denied.

The scriptures do not reveal why two years passed before Pharaoh dreamed a significant dream, but they do reveal that, as his servants were, he was troubled by his dream and had none who could interpret it: "And Pharaoh awoke, and behold it was a dream. So, in the morning his spirit was troubled, and he sent and called for all the magicians of Egypt and all its wise men. Pharaoh told them his dreams, but there was none who could interpret them to Pharaoh" (Genesis 41:7–8). It is not coincidence that Pharaoh is experiencing the same kind of dreams and emotional disturbance that the baker and the butler experienced and had no choice but to call for help if he was to have peace of mind. Unbeknown to Joseph, God was setting the stage to bring him into the fullness of his blessing.

Many times, like Joseph, while we are still sitting in our prisons of circumstance, God is setting the stage somewhere else to bring us into the fullness of the greatness He has prepared for us. Even when we can't see Him working things out, we must trust and believe that He is. Never lose sight of the fact that when God gets ready to reposition you, He will do so in such a way that only you will be able to perform in the function He has prepared. There were other wise men and magicians in the country who could interpret dreams, but only Joseph could interpret *this* dream. In the same way, there may be others in your profession with your skill or who share your knowledge, but when the time is right, only *you* will be able to perform the function.

Genesis 41:9–14 states:

> *Then the chief cupbearer said to Pharaoh, "I remember my offenses today. When Pharaoh was angry with his servants and put me and the chief baker in custody in the house of the captain of the guard, we dreamed on the same night, he and I, each having a dream with its own interpretation. A young Hebrew was there with us, a servant of the captain of the guard. When we told him, he interpreted our dreams to us, giving an interpretation to each man according to his dream. And as he interpreted to us, so it came about. I was restored to my office, and the baker was hanged." Then Pharaoh sent and called Joseph, and they quickly brought him out of the pit.*

Joseph is brought out of prison because the butler suddenly remembers Joseph's ability to interpret dreams. The same one who forgot him two years before remembers him now and is the reason for his release. We thus must never assume that people who forget us are our enemies—it simply may not yet be the season for them to remember. The challenge for us, then, is to remain constant in who we are and in what we do, until we are remembered.

When Joseph is finally placed in front of Pharaoh, he does not present a sad story in hopes of obtaining his freedom, nor does he try to deceive or trick Pharaoh to gain his own release. He is there to do what he has previously done—interpret dreams—and has the God-given ability to do. When we remain true to ourselves, especially in challenging times, we do not have to play on the sympathies of others nor play the victim of tragedy to obtain freedom from our struggles. As He did with Joseph, God will cause us and our abilities to be remembered when the season is right. We must therefore remain consistent and true to ourselves and not let ourselves be controlled by circumstance. We must remember that our blessings and outcomes are never about us but rather about the God we serve.

Until God was ready to usher Joseph into his time of greatness, Joseph had to wait in prison. Only when God was ready to cause Pharaoh to dream did the chain of events begin that would take Joseph out of prison. Thus, we should never consider our path to greater things in terms of our expected time frames. Many people quit and give up on their dreams because things did not occur when they wanted them to, but we do ourselves great disservice when we think we can achieve our life goals based solely on our skills and timelines. For example, the Bible does not tell us the amount of time that has passed from the moment Joseph's brothers attacked him until he finally appears before the king, but we can reasonably conclude that a decade or more has passed. We must therefore remember that until God causes a significant chain of events in our favor, we must endure our challenging times and prison experiences, as Joseph did.

Before coming to stand face-to-face with Pharaoh himself to once again interpret a dream, Joseph must prepare. Before being allowed to stand in the presence of the greatness of Pharaoh, Joseph is required to clean himself, shave, and change clothes: "Then Pharaoh sent and called Joseph and they quickly brought him out of the pit. And when he had shaved himself and changed his clothes, he came in before Pharaoh" (Genesis 41:14).

This principle is key on journeys toward greater things: Many people make the mistake of thinking that no change or preparation is required of us to achieve higher goals. Before we can be greater and do greater, however, we must prepare. Just as Joseph was not allowed to be in the palace while still looking and smelling like the prison, we will never be allowed to walk in the palace prepared for us by God if we are unwilling to let go of the prison mindset. Although life's problems and difficulties can leave us confined to mental, emotional, or even physical prisons, we must not allow those experiences to define who we are or to prevent us from being open to the possibility of change. To be prepared for his meeting with greatness, Joseph first had to act like he was that greatness he was about to meet. He had to shave himself and change clothes. Like Joseph, if we are looking for greater, we must act like it.

In addition to shedding the mindsets and thought processes that allowed us to survive our prisons, we must also be willing to change our clothes—the environment that surrounds us. Sometimes the people we know and the places we live can keep us looking and smelling like our prisons, and ultimately, that prevents us from being properly prepared, so we are unable to come to the palace to stand in the presence of Pharaoh.

Pharaoh here represents an opportunity for freedom. Joseph has been called by Pharaoh to help interpret his dream, but this does not guarantee his release. Joseph thus has an opportunity but not a promise. Had Joseph not been able to interpret the dream when given this opportunity, he no doubt would have been returned to prison or, even worse, put to death. We must never assume that we are promised greater simply because we are presented with an opportunity. We must also not hold the erroneous belief that life owes us something or that we are entitled to anything. Like Joseph, we must be humble in whatever state we are in until the opportunity for our release presents itself, and then when the opportunity occurs, we must maximize our advantage in the moment by preparing to be the greatness we are expecting to meet.

When asked by Pharaoh if he can interpret Pharaoh's dreams, Joseph is quick to acknowledge not his abilities but God: "And Pharaoh said to Joseph 'I have had a dream, and there is no one who can interpret it. I have heard it said of you that when you hear a dream you can interpret it.' Joseph answered Pharaoh, 'It is not in me; God will give Pharaoh a favorable answer" (Genesis 41:15–16). In this age of technology, science, and education, many people—believers and nonbelievers alike—attribute their success to their own wisdom and skill. Joseph, in contrast, understands that any skills, understandings, and wisdom he may possess are given by God.

The psalmist wrote in Psalm 111:10, "The fear of the Lord is the beginning of wisdom"; Proverbs 2:6 states, "For the Lord gives wisdom; from his mouth come knowledge and understanding"; and James 1:5 says, "If any of you lack wisdom, let him ask God, who gives generously to all without reproach, and it will be given to him." We must accept that no knowledge, skill, wisdom, or talent we have is of our own doing but is given to us by God for His good purposes. Joseph clearly points this out to Pharaoh because he wants

Pharaoh to understand that this chain of events was not of man's doing but of God's will. Although striving for and pursuing greater things and greatness are admirable goals, they are still very much allowed by the will of God. We cannot and will never be greater than the will of God will allow, nor can we attain remarkable things without Him.

Next, Pharaoh shares with Joseph the dreams that have been troubling him. Joseph not only interprets the dreams but gives Pharaoh instruction from God on how to avoid an impending famine. This so pleases Pharaoh that he elevates Joseph to a palace position:

> This proposal pleased Pharaoh and all his servants. And Pharaoh said to his servants, "Can we find a man like this, in whom is the Spirit of God?" Then Pharaoh said to Joseph, "Since God has shown you all this, there is none so discerning and wise as you are. You shall be over my house, and all my people shall order themselves as you command. Only as regards the throne will I be greater than you." And Pharaoh said to Joseph, "See, I have set you over all the land of Egypt." Then Pharaoh took his signet ring from his hand and put it on Joseph's hand, and clothed him in garments of fine linen and put a gold chain about his neck. And he made him ride in his second chariot. And they called out before him, "Bow the knee!" Thus, he set him over all the land of Egypt. Moreover, Pharaoh said to Joseph, "I am Pharaoh, and without your consent no one shall lift up hand or foot in all the land of Egypt." (Genesis 41:37–44)

In a single moment, Joseph has become second-in-command of all of Egypt. Can you imagine such a life-altering event? How can this happen? Why would an ex-con become the highest official in the land, second only to Pharaoh himself, and be given such power and authority? In answering this question, first, we must take note that Pharaoh does not place Joseph in this position because of anything that Joseph has done concerning this dream interpretation. Remember, he says to Joseph, "Since God has shown you all this, there is none so discerning and wise as you are." Because of their exchange, Pharaoh recognizes the God-given potential in Joseph. When we allow God to use us and our gifts to be blessings to others, He will allow those people to see the great potential within us, and doors will begin to open in our lives to greater things we could have never imagined.

In answering the question of how a former slave and prisoner can become second-in-command of the nation, we must next note the awesome ability of God to use anybody, no matter their current status. The fact that Joseph was a prisoner and therefore considered one of the lowest in society was irrelevant to God. God can choose the ordinary to perform the extraordinary, and the least to perform the greatest. We must never allow ourselves to think that we are not good enough or that we fail to meet any requirements to be blessed by God and to be moved into a palace assignment. No matter how bad our past or present conditions may be, and regardless of the mistakes we may have made in life, God can lead us to the palace. The fact of the matter is that our prison experiences help prepare us for the palace. Those who are on paths to greater things understand that they are always in transition and that their interlopers are but speed bumps on the way to their final destination of greatness.

Imagine what must be going through Joseph's mind when Pharaoh elevates him. He has instantly become rich in money, power, authority, and influence. He who was the least is now presiding over the greatest. Pharaoh gives him so much power that no one could come or go in all of Egypt without Joseph's permission.

When we arrive at our palace assignments, we must understand that our lives will be changed forever. Like Joseph, we will instantly find ourselves in places and positions we never could have imagined. That which we were bankrupted in while enduring difficult and hostile moments will now become abundant. People who ignored us will readily listen and will even seek out our counsel. Those who commanded us or gave us orders will now ask for our permission. Many who excluded us will beg and plead for us to briefly grace their events with our presence. Those who wronged us or otherwise treated us unfairly and unkindly will wish they had a second chance to be in our presence.

What will be required of us once we are placed in our palace assignments? Is it business as usual? Do we continue as we did prior to our elevation? When Joseph is assigned as second-in-command, Pharaoh performs two interesting acts: "And Pharaoh called Joseph's name Zaphenath-Paneah. And he gave him in marriage Asenath, the daughter of Potiphera priest of On. So Joseph went out over the land of Egypt." (Genesis 41:45). First, Pharaoh gives Joseph a new identity with his new position; no longer Joseph, he is Zaphenath-Paneah.

In this way, Pharaoh ceremoniously disconnects Joseph from any and all things related to his past. The dream killers, ditch diggers, backstabbers, and cell mates of Joseph's past have now been metaphorically released from any emotional effects that may have been still in Joseph's heart. In essence, Pharaoh is saying to Joseph, "All you have been through and all the people who put you through it no longer matter, because you are no longer that person." He is no longer Joseph, who was ridiculed for a dream, thrown into a ditch, twice sold into slavery, betrayed by a harlot, misunderstood by his master, imprisoned without cause, and forgotten about in jail, but is now Zaphenath-Paneah, second-in-command of all of Egypt. From this moment forward, his old life no longer mattered and had no bearing on his future.

Like Joseph, when we are given our palace assignments we are given new identities and are released from the things of our past, because we are no longer the people we once were. We find this principle in the scriptures. When Jesus gave the apostles their new assignments as fishers of men, he gave Simon a new identity: "One of the two who heard John speak and followed Jesus was Andrew, Simon Peter's brother. He first found his own brother Simon and said to him, 'We have found the Messiah' (which means Christ). He brought him to Jesus. Jesus looked at him and said, 'You are Simon the son of John. You shall be called Cephas' (which means Peter)" (John 1:40–42). Saul was also given a new identity with his new position as a messenger of Christ, as recorded in Acts 13:9: "But Saul, who was also called Paul, filled with the Holy Spirit, looked intently at him and said, 'You son of the devil, you enemy of all righteousness, full of all deceit and villainy, will you not stop making crooked the straight paths of the Lord?"

The second thing that Pharaoh does is give his second-in-command Asenath, the daughter of Potiphera, priest of On. In essence, he places someone in Joseph's life who will have his best interests in hand. Asenath is a servant of Pharaoh, and because of this, she undertands palace life and the requirements placed on those assigned to those positions. Likewise, when we finally arrive in our season of greater, we must find like-minded people to become part of our friend circles. We need people with us who understand the higher calling and requirements associated with greatness. All too often, we are misaligned with people who don't share our vision and passion and who ultimately hinder us and block us from reaching the place where God desires us to be. Bishop T.D. Jakes pastor of the Potter's House in Dallas, Texas, once stated in an interview that you cannot explain a giraffe's decision to a turtle because the animals' perspectives are different. Essentially, this means that many people will not understand you simply because they don't have the insight you possess or the ability to see the world as you do. It's not always easy to do, but sometimes we must stop traveling with people who are not traveling with us.

Pharaoh gives Asenath to Joseph also because he understands that Joseph cannot accomplish the tasks ahead of him on his own. We who are destined for greater recognize that no man is an island unto himself and that we all need somebody. Surrounding ourselves with people who are lazy, selfish, and unmotivated will only hinder, confound, and frustrate us. Negative people are like cancer to greatness and, once discovered, should be removed from our lives permanently. The challenge, then, is to find and attach to people who are driven, passionate, and visionary, which will only make us better.

In addition to understanding the requirements of greatness, Asenath also gives Joseph two sons: "Before the year of famine came, two sons were born to Joseph. Asenath, the daughter of Potiphera priest of On, bore them to him" (Genesis 41:50). If people in our lives are not producing for us then they are consuming from us. It is critical that we learn how to differentiate between these types of people, because it's easy to become depleted of energy, resources, and motivation when we are surrounded only by consumers, those who take from us but never give back. When we have given all we have, and yet are demanded to give more, life can become miserable, especially if we are trying to rise above mediocrity.

Joseph is given a palace assignment that comes with great responsibility; he is given the position that he told Pharaoh to create in Genesis 41:33–36:

> *Now therefore let Pharaoh select a discerning and wise man, and set him over the land of Egypt. Let Pharaoh proceed to appoint overseers over the land and take one-fifth of the produce of the land of Egypt during the seven plentiful years. And let them gather all the food of these good years that are coming and store up grain under the authority of Pharaoh for food in the cities, and let them keep it. That food shall be a reserve for the land against the seven years of famine that are to occur in the land of Egypt, so that the land may not perish through the famine.*

Here we gain insight about the preparation of Joseph. He is placed in charge of food management over all Egypt to meet the needs of the people during the upcoming seven years of severe famine. His responsibility is so great that there is no room for error; if he messes this task up, people will die and Egypt will be devastated. The task given to him is enormous, but he has been training for it for most of his life.

This is certainly not a job for someone without any leadership or management skills, and at first glance, Joseph would seem to not be qualified. A glance back at the journey that has led Joseph to this great position, however, reveals the opposite. Joseph's difficult moments have trained him for such a task. While Joseph was a slave, God used interlopers to train him for the greater that was to come. For instance, while Potiphar's slave, Joseph was in charge of all of his master's household and affairs. Nothing took place in Potiphar's house without Joseph's knowledge. Joseph was so good at his job that Potiphar would leave home for weeks at a time. This allowed Joseph to learn how to manage, supervise, and no doubt master the economics of supply and demand.

When he was eventually thrown into prison, Joseph was placed in charge of all the prisoners and of the day-to-day operations of the prison. When the baker and butler, the servants of Pharaoh, were thrown in prison, they were not assigned Joseph by accident. Although the servants of Pharaoh were being punished, they were still to be treated almost as royalty, so only the best prisoners could be assigned as their servants, so when Joseph met them, it was as a leader entrusted to oversee the well-being of Pharaoh's property. During the most difficult times of his life, then, Joseph was being trained for the greater that was coming. When he was finally selected for this great challenge by Pharaoh himself, Joseph was not without skills or experience; rather, his resume was full of accomplishments. Pharaoh entrusted him to oversee the well-being of Pharaoh's property, something Joseph was already doing in prison.

When we, like Joseph, are given our palace assignments, we will be given great responsibility, but we must understand that we will have already been trained, prepared, and ordained for our tasks by the difficult people and disturbing moments we have faced in our lives. Many people miss this principle as they seek greater for their own selfish reasons. The truth is, those of us on a path to greater lives understand that the journey is not for personal gain. Joseph was made second-in-command not so he would relish and flaunt his power and promote prosperity teachings and lavish lifestyles, but rather so he could make the lives of others better. Joseph was able to be a servant and minister to the needs of the people. Being great is never about the power and authority given to us but rather what we do with it to help others around us.

We must trust that when our season comes, we will be ready to meet the challenge, for we, like Joseph, will have been prepared by the interlopers that God placed in our lives to prepare us for the greater things He has in store for us.

6

Lessons from Joseph

In the final analysis, Joseph's life has not been easy such as the television show portrayal of the lifestyles of the rich and famous. One would miss or overlook the struggles he faced by focusing solely on his palace life. Many times, people judge and misunderstand us by assuming we are the sum total of a particular season of life. If we were to know Joseph only in context of the position, power, prosperity, and privilege afforded him because of his palace assignment, we could easily presume that he was an aristocrat who related only to the elite in society. But we know much more about Joseph. We know that although he did rise to greatness, it was not because of an elitist lifestyle but rather because of interlopers who helped prepare and lead him there. We can glean from his life some very powerful and beneficial lessons, especially for those destined for the greater things that life has in store.

Lesson 1: "God Is In Control of The Process"

Many people want to achieve and accomplish remarkable things, but very few want to go through the process by which these goals are attained. Our society and culture teach us and condition us to believe that faster is better. The advent of technology has destroyed patience; whatever we desire can be ours in a matter of days or minutes, if not seconds. The process by which God leads us to the greater things in life is not always easy, simple, or expeditious.

Joseph's journey from the pit to the palace was difficult, to say the least, and many would have given up along the way. If we are going to achieve greater things in life and walk in a season of greatness, we must understand that achieving greatness is never an overnight task but is a process. The process that leads us to the places destined for us is usually a series of ups and downs and a series of interactions with people who may not have our best interests at heart.

By design, God's process always comes with purpose. Even when we don't understand the purpose, we must trust the process. As Joseph did, we will see a season of suffering before any season of success. Many people look for success, but they don't always understand the suffering that sometimes accompanies this challenge. God understood that, were He to give Joseph the palace position prematurely, Joseph would not have been able to handle the assignment. This is why it takes some people years to achieve success in a particular career or life's ambition: They had to go through the process so they would not mishandle the greater things God had in place for them. When God is directing our paths, it can be difficult to understand the process because we are usually looking with man's understanding. We must not look to our understanding to understand God, as Proverbs 3:5 reminds us: "Trust in the Lord with all your heart, and do not lean on your own understanding." Interlopers in our lives help prepare us in ways we sometimes cannot see until the desired goal has been achieved.

Joseph had a dream that one day he would rule over his family, but that dream did not contain the pit, slavery, Potiphar's wife, the prison, or the servants of Pharaoh. This principle is important to remember; we must understand that when we are destined for greater things, we will have the vision to see ourselves doing great works, but usually, the vision will be void of the process. During the civil rights movement, Dr. Martin Luther King Jr. dreamed of seeing his children one day being judged not by the color of their skin but by the content of their character, but that dream was void of the struggle against Jim Crow laws, bus boycotts, attack with water hoses and vicious dogs, senseless lynching's of blacks in the south, and even his own incarceration and eventual assassination.

It is also imperative that we consider that the process we go through on our way to greatness is not ours to determine but rather God's: "For I know thoughts that I think toward you, saith the Lord, thoughts of peace, and not of evil, to give you an expected end" (Jeremiah 29:11; KJV). It is God who determines the courses of those being prepared for the greater things ahead. It is therefore a challenge for us to not lose sight of our dreams, hopes, and goals because of the process. We must not forget that the process is crucial for our preparation and that the interlopers in our lives—whether difficult people or stressful dilemmas—are a necessary part of that process by which God takes us to the next level and, ultimately, to the greater things in store for us.

Lesson 2: "God Is Always with Us"

It would be a mistake to assume that God forsakes us and allows us to navigate the most difficult moments of life alone. It's hard to see God working on our behalf while our eyes are flooded with tears. Likewise, we cannot always feel the presence of God through our pain and can mistakenly contribute the void we feel during those times to divine neglect. When our circumstances are astringent enough, they can cause us to struggle in our faith and belief:

> *And they brought the boy to him. And when the spirit saw him, immediately it convulsed the boy, and he fell on the ground and rolled about, foaming at the mouth. And Jesus asked his father, "How long has this been happening to him?" And he said, "From childhood. And it has often cast him into fire and into water, to destroy him. But if you can do anything, have compassion on us and help us." And Jesus said to him, " 'If you can'! All things are possible for one who believes." Immediately the father of the child cried out and said, "I believe; help my unbelief!"*

(Mark 9:20–24)

When we can allow ourselves to fully accept that God is always with us, the difficult people and times are easier to endure. We must understand that nothing happens to us without God's permission. Consider the life of Job. All that occurred in Job's life happened only because God allowed it:

> *And the Lord said to Satan, "Have you considered my servant Job, that there is none like him on the earth, a blameless and upright man, who fears God and turns away from evil? He still holds fast his integrity, although you incited me against him to destroy him without reason." Then Satan answered the Lord and said, "Skin for skin! All that a man has he will give*

> *for his life. But stretch out your hand and touch his bone and his flesh, and he will curse you to your face." And the Lord said to Satan, "Behold, he is in your hand; only spare his life." So, Satan went out from the presence of the Lord and struck Job with loathsome sores from the sole of his foot to the crown of his head.*
>
> (Job 2:3–7)

Although God did not plan or perform the terrible things that befell Job, He certainly did approve, allow, and give permission for them to happen. If we are to ever rise above the difficult people and crises that befall us, we must understand that, regardless of how random the experience may seem, it is always with the permission of God, who has promised in Hebrews 13:5 to never leave us or forsake us. Even Christ himself assures us that He will always be with us: "Go therefore and make disciples of all nations, baptizing them in the name of the Father and of the Son and of the Holy Spirit, teaching them to observe all that I have commanded you. And behold, I am with you always, to the end of the age" (Matthew 28:19–20).

We saw this principle again and again in Joseph's story. From the moment Joseph was sold into slavery, the scriptures tell us that God was with him, from each perilous moment to the next. As a matter of fact, it was because of God that Joseph was able to endure each of his hardships and, more importantly, to prosper and be successful in them. When we understand that God is always with us no matter how bad or good the conditions of our lives are, getting through those dark times becomes more tolerable because we have peace of mind and comfort in knowing that we are not facing our trials and tribulations alone.

Lesson 3: "The Joseph Factor"

Joseph had a unique quality that caused some to be endeared to him yet others to despise him. Although the Bible does not give us many specifics about Joseph's character, we can glean hints about his demeanor and personage based on his actions. From the beginning of his story, no matter who he met, Joseph had the uncanny ability to affect people on an emotional level while he himself remained content while facing overwhelming struggles. This ability can be termed the Joseph factor. People who have Joseph factor have an innate ability to either draw people near or drive them away. It can be both a curse and a blessing because people with the Joseph factor, like Joseph, are subjected to the whims of others based on their emotional reactions to us. Joseph's brothers hated him without cause, and subsequently, they mistreated him and plotted his demise.

The Joseph factor is not quite the same as charisma. What made Joseph unique was his ability to remain humble, content, and even-tempered in whatever situation he found himself in. People on a journey to a greater destiny have learned that the challenge is not gaining control over any given situation but maintaining self-control at any given time. Joseph was a master of his emotions. If there was ever a time he was truly frustrated, sad, bitter, or even vengeful, the scriptures do not reveal it. When his family threw him in the pit, we are not told that he returned their ill will with the same malicious intent. When his brothers sold him into slavery, the scriptures do not show that he fought back or even attempted to escape. What the scriptures do reveal is that because of his consistent demeanor and personality, each person Joseph had an encounter with was affected in one way or another. This ability to deal with others beyond face value is crucial to those of us seeking greater things. Regardless of how people treat us we must learn to master humility in our response to them.

Potiphar, his wife, the prison officials, Pharaoh's servants, and Pharaoh himself are all drawn to Joseph for different reasons. The scriptures state that some of them readily identified the Spirit of God with him: "His master saw that the Lord was with him" (Genesis 39:3); "But the Lord was with Joseph and showed him steadfast love and gave him favor in the sight of the keeper of the prison" (Genesis 39:21); and "Then Pharaoh said to Joseph, 'Since God has shown you all this, there is none so discerning and wise as you are' " (Genesis 41:39).

When the Joseph factor resides in us, it will cause others to see the potential for greatness in us but also, and more importantly, the presence of the hand of God in our lives. Joseph's behavior, demeanor, attitude, and response to the difficult people and moments in his life were the sole reasons for his ability to master them.

The Joseph factor will cause people to be drawn to you or, in abject hatred of the good in you, to be driven away from you. Either way, we must understand it's not really a characteristic of ours but rather the God in us that causes these reaction in others. Average people, those satisfied with mediocrity, do not possess the Joseph factor and usually lack the self-control required to obtain greatness. Many people would not have been able to maintain Joseph's demeanor and positive attitude throughout his ordeal. Some would have fought back, engaged in heated verbal exchanges, used inappropriate language, perhaps tried to escape, and even abused the powers and freedoms they had while incarcerated, thus preventing them from coming into the greater things God had in store.

As we see in Romans 12:17–21, Paul understood that the Joseph factor is inclusive of how we react to the interlopers in our lives: "Repay no one evil for evil, but give thought to do what is honorable in the sight of all. If possible, so far as it depends on you, live peaceably with all. Beloved, never avenge yourselves, but leave it to the wrath of God, for it is written, 'Vengeance is mine, I will repay, says the Lord.' To the contrary, 'if your enemy is hungry, feed him; if he is thirsty, give him something to drink; for by so doing you will heap burning coals on his head.' Do not be overcome by evil, but overcome evil with good."

Lesson 4: "The Change Within"

The process that leads us from the pit to the palace will ultimately change us in ways we cannot imagine. Most things that don't kill us make us stronger, and we are often wiser after difficult moments than before we endured them. Therefore, the process that God sets for us is so important to our preparation for our season of greater. The Joseph who is assigned as second-in-command over all of Egypt is fundamentally different from the Joseph who helped his brothers watch over his father's flock as a boy. While we are being prepared and led to the greater things, we are being transformed.

After Joseph has reached greatness, his brothers come before him to seek assistance; amazingly, they don't recognize him: "Now Joseph was governor over the land. He was the one who sold to all the people of the land. And Joseph's brothers came and bowed themselves before him with their faces to the ground. Joseph saw his brothers and recognized them, but he treated them like strangers and spoke roughly to them. 'Where do you come from?' he said. They said, 'From the land of Canaan, to buy food.' And Joseph recognized his brothers, but they did not recognize him" (Genesis 42:6–8). Many times, people cannot perceive the change that has occurred within us, even though we have been so fundamentally changed by our journeys that we don't think, act, or respond as we once did. Sometimes, as in the case of Joseph, that those who once knew us no longer recognize us. When Joseph's brothers come before him, he is no longer the humble, quaint, and passive littler brother that they used to mistreat, overlook, and abuse. As second-in-command of the house of Pharaoh, he is acts with confidence, authority, and purpose. He is so fundamentally different internally that his own flesh and blood don't recognize him.

Like Joseph's brothers, people who once perceived us a certain way will no longer be able to relate to us after we have come into our season of greatness. This is not necessarily because we think we are better than they or that they are beneath us (which sometimes happens) but rather because we are no longer the people they assume still exist. Joseph's brothers' last memory of him was of throwing him in the pit and selling him into slavery, so they would only be able to see and relate to him as a slave. They cannot imagine him in any other position in life, so when they stand before him, seeking assistance, they know him not. Likewise, some people in our lives can only see and relate to us if we are helpless, enslaved, or imprisoned so instead of dealing with us as royalty in the palace, they approach us as inmates in prison. They could never imagine us in any other position in life, so that when our paths cross again, we are foreign to them.

It can be very challenging to relate to people who no longer know and understand us the way they once did, so that now, we must justify and explain everything we do or say. The challenge for us, then, is to not lower ourselves to their level but to bring them up to ours. We must help people to understand that we are no longer who we were in the pit, as Joseph does with his brothers:

> *Then Joseph could not control himself before all those who stood by him. He cried, "Make everyone go out from me." So, no one stayed with him when Joseph made himself known to his brothers. And he wept aloud, so that the Egyptians heard it, and the household of Pharaoh heard it. And Joseph said to his brothers, "I am Joseph! Is my father still alive?" But his brothers could not answer him, for they were dismayed at his presence. So, Joseph said to his brothers, "Come near to me, please." And they came near. And he said, "I am your brother, Joseph, whom you sold into Egypt. And now do not be distressed or*

angry with yourselves because you sold me here, for God sent me before you to preserve life. So it was not you who sent me here, but God."

(Genesis 45:1–5)

Because his brothers cannot understand the ways he has been transformed, Joseph brings them to a place of understanding. We who are doing greater should never abandon people who can't comprehend who we have become or our new places in life. Like Joseph, we should help them understand the new purpose and passion in our lives caused by our new positions.

People who have wronged, criticized, mistreated, and perhaps lied about us will find themselves dismayed at our new assignment. Joseph understands this and therefore helps his brothers understand that while their actions were meant for bad God allowed them for His purposes. This is important because when we realize that when bad things or the evil acts of others happen to us are allowed by God, then we shouldn't seek revenge or wish ill will toward our interlopers. Like Joseph, we should understand that it is God who allows the difficulties into our life.

Joseph even takes care of his entire family after they are reunited. He allows them to know that no matter what they intended for him, God used them as interlopers that led him to a higher calling and position in life:

And they sent a messenger unto Joseph, saying, Thy father did command before he died, saying, So shall ye say unto Joseph, Forgive, I pray thee now, the trespass of thy brethren, and their sin; for they did unto thee evil: and now, we pray thee, forgive the trespass of the servants of the God of thy father. And Joseph wept when they spake unto him. And his brethren also went and fell down before his face; and they said, Behold, we be thy servants. And Joseph said unto them, Fear not: for am I in the place of God? But as for you, ye thought evil against me; but God meant it unto good, to bring to pass, as it is this day, to save much people alive. Now therefore fear ye not: I will nourish you, and your little ones. And he comforted them, and spake kindly unto them.

(Genesis 50:16–21)

Those who are on journeys to greater things have an awesome responsibility to understand what others don't. They also have the ability to see the big picture. In spite of all the evil things his brothers did to him, for example, Joseph understood that he was where God had appointed him to be for a greater purpose, and that all he had endured at his brothers' hands had happened because God had allowed it. When we understand this, we will be able, like Joseph, to nourish people and add value to their lives regardless of how they have treated us, because in the final summation, our path of greatness is really not about us but about doing the will of God.

Interlopers help prepare us for the greater things assigned by God to our lives and help transform us into whom God wants us to be. We must therefore take comfort when dealing with difficult people and enduring hard times, knowing, trusting, and believing that God is allowing these people and hard times to be in our lives so His will in our lives will be done. No matter where you are right now on your journey, let Joseph's story serve as a reminder that if you remain faithful, your ending will become greater than your beginning: "And Pharaoh said to Joseph, See, I have set you over all the land of Egypt." (Genesis. 41:41).

The Cure
From your tiredness
is intimacy with Jesus

* the past woo neverending
* the Abuse/Yes hurt
  the Rape/Yes wrong and violation
         to your body mind, body
               & Spirit

who it
plan By Lord NO
Will it Be use by God yes
to prepare you for the Break
 Prepare Lord who for your
        life

CPSIA information can be obtained
at www.ICGtesting.com
Printed in the USA
LVHW081446120621
690002LV00024B/1032